Community Helpers

Teachers

by Cari Meister

Bullfrog Books

Ideas for Parents and Teachers

Bullfrog Books let children practice reading informational text at the earliest reading levels. Repetition, familiar words, and photo labels support early readers.

Before Reading

- Discuss the cover photo. What does it tell them?

- Look at the picture glossary together. Read and discuss the words.

Read the Book

- "Walk" through the book and look at the photos. Let the child ask questions. Point out the photo labels.

- Read the book to the child, or have him or her read independently.

After Reading

- Prompt the child to think more. Ask: What else does your teacher do? Would you like to be a teacher? Why or why not?

Bullfrog Books are published by Jump!
5357 Penn Avenue South
Minneapolis, MN 55419
www.jumplibrary.com

Library of Congress Cataloging-in-Publication Data
Meister, Cari.
  Teachers / by Cari Meister.
    pages cm.—(Bullfrog Books: Community Helpers)
  Includes bibliographical references and index.
  Summary: "This photo-illustrated book for early readers gives examples of what teachers teach, and what they do before and after school"—Provided by publisher.
  ISBN 978-1-62031-079-3 (hardcover:alk. paper)
  ISBN 978-1-62496-035-2 (ebook)
  1. Teachers—Juvenile literature. I. Title.
  LB1775.M497 2014
  371.1--dc23
                                    2012044155

Series Editor: Rebecca Glaser
Series Designer: Ellen Huber
Book Designer: Lindaanne Donohoe
Photo Researcher: Kurtis Kinneman

Photo Credits: Corbis, 12–13, 16–17, 18–19, 23bl; iStockphoto, 1, 4, 14, 21, 23tl; Lindaanne Donohoe, 9, 23br; Shutterstock, 3, 5, 6–7, 8, 10 (inset), 10–11, 15, 19, 20t, 20b, 22, 23rt, 24; SuperStock, cover

Printed in the United States of America at Corporate Graphics in North Mankato, Minnesota.
5-2013 / PO 1003
10 9 8 7 6 5 4 3 2 1

Table of Contents

Teachers at Work

Ty wants to be a teacher.

What do they do?

Teachers help kids learn.

Miss Bart goes to school early.

She works on a lesson plan.

lesson plan

Subject: Language Arts
Grade: Grade 1
Topic: Words and Actions
Content: Vocabulary for key classroom words

Goals	Students will learn the names of objects in the classroom. They will also be able to understand classroom directions.
Objectives	The students will match pictures to objects to the object by placing picture cards next to the object. After listening to a direction given by the teacher, the student will follow that direction by correctly completing the action.
Materials	Children's dictionaries and dictionary cards with pictures
Introduction	Ask questions to see what vocabulary students know.
Development	Using the dictionary as a reference, I will model the actions. Students will follow along in their own dictionaries. Then students will model the actions as they say each word.
Practice	Students will repeat the vocabulary after me while looking at the picture, or the actual object. Students will work with a partner. They will ask each other questions about the classroom. They will give each other directions.
Understanding	Listen to the children pronounce the vocabulary. Ask the students to "act out" the directions.
Closure	Review the vocabulary words. Assign practice work at home.

Mrs. Dare is teaching reading.

She points to words.

Amir reads them.

Mr. Su is teaching science.

Jon has a question.

Mr. Su helps him
understand.

Mr. Rue's class is on a field trip.

They learn about the woods.

They find a bird nest.

Mrs. Peck teaches gym class.

She teaches game rules.

She shows kids how to play fair.

The bell rings.
School is over.
Mr. Lee stays late.
He grades homework.

Teachers do good work!

In the Classroom

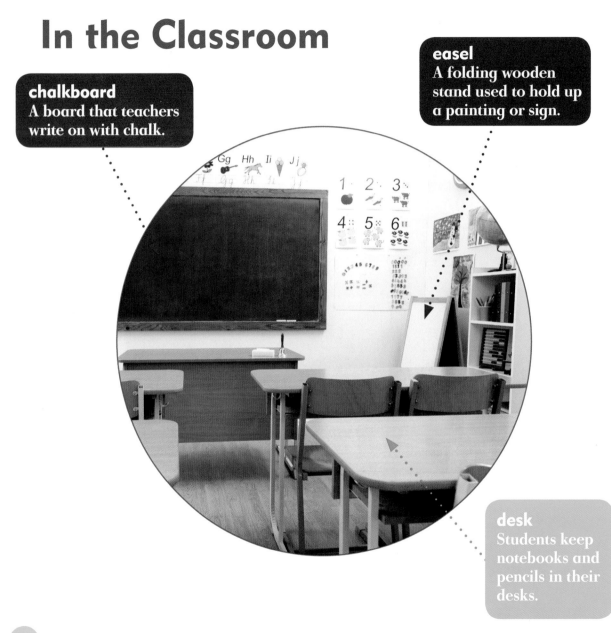

easel
A folding wooden stand used to hold up a painting or sign.

chalkboard
A board that teachers write on with chalk.

desk
Students keep notebooks and pencils in their desks.

Picture Glossary

field trip
A trip away from school to learn about something.

homework
Work given by a teacher to be done away from school.

gym class
A class where kids learn about games, sports, and fitness.

lesson plan
A guide made by a teacher to explain how a subject will be taught.

Index

To Learn More

Learning more is as easy as 1, 2, 3.

1) Go to www.factsurfer.com

2) Enter "teachers" into the search box.

3) Click the "Surf" button to see a list of websites.

With factsurfer.com, finding more information is just a click away.